WHEN YOU LOSE
SOMEONE YOU LOVE

A Book of Comfort and Hope

by

Richard Exley

Tulsa, Oklahoma

Janette
My Best Friend
& the sister I never
had as a Child —
Love you,
Winnie
10/'96

PRESENTED TO

Janette

in memory of

your Mom

No pain is greater than that which you experience following the death of one you love. Many times you are isolated with your sorrow. No one seems to understand what you are experiencing, and those who do are often at a loss for words. Not infrequently you are separated by long distances from those who would love and support you in your time of loss. Please accept this small book, not as a substitute for our presence, but as an expression of our deepest love and continuing concern for you in your time of grief.

from

Winnie, Don, Paul & Elizabeth

When You Lose Someone You Love
A Book of Comfort and Hope
ISBN 1-56292-111-8
Copyright © 1995 and 1991 by Richard Exley
7807 East 76th Street
Tulsa, Oklahoma 74133-3648

Published by Honor Books
P.O. Box 55388
Tulsa, Oklahoma 74155

DEDICATION

To all those men and women who, in their grief, taught me not only how to grieve, but how to find the comfort of God.

CONTENTS

NOTE TO THE READER

Since I have written this book in the form of letters addressed to "Peter," I think it is only fair to tell you that Peter is not a real person. He is, rather, a composite of all the grieving people I have worked with during the past twenty-five years. Because the individuals from whom the composite was constructed are real, the questions Peter raises and the issues he deals with in regard to the death of his beloved are also very real.

I have chosen the "letter style" because it affords me the opportunity to speak to you directly and in a much more personal manner. This is not a book about grief; rather, it is comfort extended to those who are even now walking through "the valley of the shadow of death."

In order to protect the privacy of those grieving persons with whom I have worked, I have taken the liberty of changing their names, and, in some instances, have altered specific details regarding their loss. However, the reality of their grief and the concerns to which it gave birth have been preserved as accurately as my memory affords.

"Then the end will come, when he [Christ] hands over the kingdom to God the Father after he has destroyed all dominion, authority and power. For he must reign until he has put all his enemies under his feet. The last enemy to be destroyed is death."

1 Corinthians 15:24-26

The First Letter

WHEN DEATH COMES

Dear Peter:

How often I think of the loss of your beloved and the anguished grief to which it gave birth. The initial moments have been indelibly imprinted upon my mind. I can still see you smiling bravely as you rose to greet me when I came to give what comfort I could. Somehow that brave smile was even more heartrending than the sobs which came later. Even in the moment of your loss, you still wanted to be the caregiver; you wanted to make my task easier.

In your grief you said that you felt handicapped, that you had never had to deal with anything like this before. How right you are. Nothing in life really prepares us for the death of a loved one, especially if that death is totally unexpected. Although we know that many people, even children, die every day, we never think it can happen in our family — and with good reason, for it has been estimated that the average person can go through a twenty-year period without being exposed to the death of a single relative or friend.

Still, sooner or later all of us are confronted with the inevitable. It may come unexpectedly. A phone call, in the dead of night, notifies us of our brother's sudden death. A uniformed police officer quietly informs us of a fatal auto accident involving our son or daughter. Or it may come as the long-awaited blow at the end of a lengthy illness. However death comes, it is always painful and inevitably followed by grief and an almost overwhelming sense of loss.

I won't pretend that I know entirely what you are feeling or that I can fully comprehend the depth of your grief. Nor will I pretend that I have all the answers to your tormenting questions. In truth, all I really have to share is my love and the painful lessons I have learned while dealing with my own grief and while helping others deal with theirs.

My first experience with death came when I was just a boy of nine. Mother was taken to the hospital some time in the middle of the night, and Grandma Exley came to stay with my two brothers and me. For the next two and a half days Mother struggled to give birth to her fourth child. She succeeded only after the doctors performed a Caesarean section. I was too young to understand any of this, but I can remember the laughter and cheers when Grandma told us that we had a baby sister. In minutes we were announcing to the neighborhood.

Some time later, Dad came home and gathered us three boys around him. He was bowed with weariness and grief. With great difficulty he told us the painful news. Yes, Mother had given birth to a daughter, our long-awaited sister, but things didn't look good. She was a hydrocephalic baby and wasn't expected to live. Even if she did live, she would never be normal.

Tears were running down Dad's cheeks when he finished, and I seemed to be smothering; I couldn't get my breath. I sat there numbly for a minute more, then I burst off the couch and ran through the dining room and kitchen, choking on my sobs. The screen door slammed against the house with a frightful racket as I flung it open and stumbled down the back steps toward the garage.

For the better part of the next hour, I lay with my face buried in the dirt floor. Great heaving sobs convulsed my small frame, and it seemed everything in the universe withdrew, leaving me alone with my pain. The dusty floor mingled with my tears, becoming mud, and I pounded my fists into the ground until I had no strength left. After a long while, my grief seemed to exhaust itself, leaving me with a hollow feeling in the pit of my stomach.

I think I accepted Carolyn's death that afternoon, though it was not to become a reality until just before Christmas, three months hence. The intervening weeks were filled with several crises. Once, Dad and Aunt Elsie made a flying trip to the children's hospital in Denver.

When they arrived, Carolyn was critical, at the point of death. The doctors were able to stabilize her condition, and after she had spent some days in the hospital, we brought her home for the last time. I can just vaguely remember Mother placing her in my lap, as I sat in the armchair, and watching with a painful love as I fed her a few ounces of formula.

It seemed each day brought some new disappointment. Soon we realized that Carolyn was both blind and deaf, and her head, larger than the rest of her tiny body at birth, became increasingly disproportionate. With a pain that lingers still, I remember watching Mother day by day as she bathed Carolyn tenderly, then carefully measuring her head to see if, by some miracle, it was any smaller. It never was. Mama would bite her lip then, while silent tears ran down her cheeks as she carefully put away the cloth tape measure.

Carolyn died in her sleep, at home, early one morning. Our family doctor and Aunt Elsie arrived at about the same time. He, to make the official diagnosis, and Aunt

5

Elsie to fix breakfast, which no one ate, and to see after us boys. A short time later, the mortician came and took Carolyn's tiny body away, and the gray December day passed in a maze of necessary activities.

The funeral service and trip to the cemetery have been completely blocked from my memory, leaving me without a single detail. I do, however, remember eating supper after the funeral. Grief rendered the food tasteless, but we ate anyway, mechanically, out of some misbegotten sense of obligation. We ate in the kitchen with one small lamp the only light. It left deep shadows around the table, shadows which matched the sorrow in our hearts. To this day I cannot remember a sadder meal.

As a child I was able to accept Carolyn's death without affixing responsibility. It was enough to know that she was with Jesus, in heaven, where there is no more sickness or pain, no more sorrow or crying. By Christmas her death was already becoming a painful but fading memory.

The questions came later, after I became a pastor and found myself ministering to families in similar situations.

Their desperate questions gave birth to my own: Was God to blame for Carolyn's death? Did He kill her, or at least allow her to die? Questions like these drove me to my knees. Desperately I searched the Scriptures for understanding.

After months of painful agonizing, I concluded that sin, not God, is responsible for disease and death. That is not to say Carolyn's death was the result of her own personal sin, or even, God forbid, the sin of her parents; rather, it means that sin has tainted the entire human race and that disease and death are the inevitable consequences. Romans 5:12 (KJV) declares: "Wherefore, as by one man sin entered into the world, and death by sin; and so death passed upon all men...."

In my counseling with those who question why humans must suffer, sometimes I simplistically explain that we inhabit a planet which is in rebellion, that we are part of a race who are living outside of God's will, and that one consequence of that rebellion is sickness and death. God doesn't send this plague upon people, nor does He will it.

It is simply a natural consequence of humanity's fallen state. Although, as believers, we are a new creation in Christ (2 Corinthians 5:17), we remain a part of this human family — a family which is tainted by sin and death. As a consequence, we too suffer the inevitable repercussions of that fallen state, though we are personally committed to the doing of God's will and the coming of His kingdom.

In truth, the cause of sickness and death is not God, but the hated enemy, sin. Not our personal sin necessarily, not a specific sin — for life and death cannot be reduced to a mathematical equation — but the fact of sin.

Jesus addressed the relationship between personal sin and death in Luke 13:1-5:

> *Now there were some present at that time who told Jesus about the Galileans whose blood Pilate had mixed with their sacrifices. Jesus answered, "Do you think that these Galileans were worse sinners than all the other Galileans because they suffered this way? I tell you, no!....*

> *Or those eighteen who died when the tower in Siloam fell on them — do you think they were more guilty than all the others living in Jerusalem? I tell you, no!..."*

Jesus does not tell us why these particular individuals died while others equally sinful were allowed to live, but He does make it clear that the reason for their deaths is far more complicated than mere cause and effect.

As you well know, Peter, when death strikes a loved one unexpectedly, we long for a reason, an explanation, but often there is none. In desperation we try to make some sense out of it, but often there are simply no pat answers, no ready conclusions. In times like these we must always resist the temptation to speak where God has not spoken. Beyond the simple explanation that death comes as a result of humanity's sinful state, God has not given us any insight into the "why" of individual deaths.

In many ways, Peter, death remains a mystery, even to the Christian: Why is one child taken in infancy and not another? Why is a good man stricken in the prime of life,

9

leaving behind a wife and children, while other vicious and cruel men live to a ripe old age? Why? Why? Why? The questions are almost endless, and I must admit that I am often without answers, but of this one thing I am sure — God is not to blame! In fact, when tragedy strikes, when a loved one dies, God's heart is the first of all hearts to break!

In His Comfort,

The Second Letter

WITHOUT WARNING

"Who shall separate us from the love of Christ?...I am convinced that neither death nor life, neither angels nor demons, neither the present nor the future, nor any powers, neither height nor depth, nor anything else in all creation, will be able to separate us from the love of God that is in Christ Jesus our Lord."

Romans 8:35,38,39

WITHOUT WARNING

Dear Peter:

In my first letter I talked about the unspeakable pain of losing someone we love and the inevitable questions which always accompany their death. Although I did not address your situation directly, I trust that you found the universal truths about God's faithfulness and compassion helpful. For my part I am strengthened, somehow, when I know that God shares my pain. The knowledge of His nearness does not render my grief painless, but it does give me the strength to bear it.

"Death," as Joe Bayly so aptly put it, "is a wound to the living."[1] Yet, like all wounds, some deaths are more severe than others. For instance, the death of a child is more painful than that of an aged parent. And an unexpected

13

death is almost always more traumatic than one which comes at the conclusion of a lengthy illness.

As a pastor for nearly twenty-five years, I have had numerous occasions to walk with families through "the valley of the shadow of death." I have wept with parents following the accidental death of a beloved son. I have held the hand of a grieving widow as she tried to imagine life without her husband of nearly fifty years. And I have stood beside a tiny grave with a grief-stricken couple who laid their stillborn child to rest. Although every experience of death is unique in its own way, in another sense all grief experiences have many things in common.

With your permission I would like to relate a tragic experience which I think may help you to understand better your own grief. It involves the unexpected death of a 23-year-old woman following a brief illness. Her family had no warning and no time to prepare for their tragic loss. In that sense their experience is not unlike your own, and, like you, they were left reeling. One minute they were a happy family, and the next moment their world was shattered.

Their daughter's fatal illness began innocently enough one evening with a headache which grew more severe as the night progressed. Twice the young woman telephoned her sister Corrie who prayed with her and told her to try and get some sleep.

Later, after the extent of the illness had become known, Corrie told me she had considered getting up and going to her sister's apartment but had decided against it. Sherry, she had reasoned, was a registered nurse and was fully capable of taking care of herself. Besides, it was probably just a migraine headache — extremely painful, but not dangerous.

There had been no more calls that night, and Corrie awoke in the morning feeling somewhat the worse for wear, but relieved. Routinely she prepared breakfast and got her girls off to school. By mid-morning her house was straightened and she thought of calling her sister, but decided against it. Sherry, she reasoned, had had a rough

15

night and was undoubtedly getting some much-needed rest.

When she hadn't telephoned by noon, Corrie decided to go by her apartment and see how she was feeling. After ringing the doorbell several times without getting a response, she used her key to let herself in. Anxiously she called, "Sherry?" When there was no answer, her anxiety deepened. Moving into the bedroom, she noticed that the bed was unmade, but empty. Then she heard soft moans coming from the bathroom where she discovered Sherry, on the floor, unconscious.

Rushing to her side, she tried to arouse her, but to no avail. Quickly she dialed 911 and requested an ambulance. While waiting for the paramedics to arrive, she called her husband who, in turn, called me. I arrived at the hospital just minutes after the ambulance and spent the next hour comforting the family while the doctors performed a battery of tests on the still-unconscious Sherry.

After what seemed an eternity, the doctor came in looking grim. "The diagnosis is not good," he explained to

Corrie. "Your sister has spinal meningitis and is now in a coma. We are moving her upstairs into the intensive care unit. If her condition continues to deteriorate, we will have to place her on a life-support system."

Corrie collapsed into her husband's arms and sobbed for several minutes. With a determined effort she got hold of herself and took charge. Phone calls were made to family and friends, locally and across the nation. As word of the crisis spread, Christian friends began coming to the hospital to offer comfort and encouragement. Within hours the family arrived from out of state, and the vigil was underway.

For the next two and one-half days we virtually lived at the hospital. Exhausting hours were spent in the intensive care waiting room, interrupted only by brief visits to Sherry's bedside. Her room was deathly quiet, the only sound the soft whoosh of the breathing machine. Occasionally her mother, or Corrie, would kneel by the bed to pray, or to softly plead with her to get well, all to no avail. Her condition remained unchanged.

17

Slowly, reality began to sink in. Sherry was not going to recover apart from a miracle. With that knowledge, our prayers took on a new urgency, then a certain desperation, and finally a painful resignation. Then the inevitable moment came. After consultation with the doctors, the decision was reached. There was no reason to continue to pretend that Sherry was alive. In truth, she was already dead. There was absolutely no trace of brain activity, and there hadn't been for two days. With no little sadness, the medical staff disconnected the life-support system, and the family struggled to accept the unacceptable.

Life continued, but with a certain surrealism. The tragic truth was simply too painful to be comprehended, just as it was too real to be denied. A healthy 23-year-old woman doesn't just suddenly contract a deadly disease and die — not in America, not in the 1980s, not with all of the advances made by modern medical science. Yet, Sherry had, and she had died. Her body was being prepared for burial, and her stunned loved ones were tearfully planning the funeral.

The Second Letter

As atypical as Sherry's death was, the grief experienced by her loved ones was not unlike that which follows every death. As you may well recall from your own experience, Peter, bereavement is first encountered as a shock which somehow numbs the pain.

You feel as if you have been swathed in great bands of cotton. You continue to comprehend reality and interact with the world, but as if from a great distance. Life goes on, but in slow motion. Everything seems to be filtered through layers and layers of insulation.

You can probably remember how the first two or three days passed in a maze of necessary details, which served to distance you from the reality of the death even as you seemed to be dealing with it. The details themselves became a sort of mandatory escape, a legitimate way of postponing the full force of your grief.

Every decision took on a special significance: What should your beloved be buried in? Who should you ask to give the eulogy? What scriptures should be read and who should conduct the service? Should you have the service in the funeral home or in the church? Should it be held in the morning or afternoon? What about special music? Should you accept flowers or establish a memorial fund? Who should pick out the casket and the burial plot? The list went on and on.

Peter, now that you are a few weeks removed from the loss of your beloved, can you step back from your pain and get a glimpse of the whole picture? Can you see how compassionate God is? Due to humanity's sinfulness, He cannot yet totally eradicate death, but He can and does make it somehow bearable.

The shock which we experience initially is His way of helping us deal with the pain of our loss. It works like a divine tranquilizer which enables us to comprehend the reality of death without plummeting the full depth of our devastating loss. As the initial shock wears off, the promise of eternal life with our departed loved one becomes the gift of hope which keeps us going until grief has done its healing work.

After the funeral, life returns to something akin to normal for most of your family and friends, but not for you. For you, grief's long journey is just beginning. Long after the last casserole has been devoured and the serving dishes washed and returned, long after the last of your out-of-town relatives have said their good-byes and made the long journey home, long after your most caring friends have recovered from their grief and resumed a normal life, you are still grieving. The pain of your loss lingers like a stubborn toothache.

And now, more than ever, you need the ministry of comfort. Not covered dishes and sympathy cards, but a safe place with a safe person, somewhere you can grieve without being rebuked, or even misunderstood. You need someone who will let you be real, someone who will let you weep or rage as the case may be. Someone who won't try to explain the unexplainable, or "fix" everything with a prayer.

In my next letter, Peter, we'll talk about the healing power of grief. Until then, know that you are loved and that the things you are feeling are "normal" for someone who has lost a loved one.

One final suggestion: Don't let anyone make you feel guilty because you are still grieving. Grief is a slow process and often takes as long as two years to complete its healing work. That doesn't mean that you will always hurt this badly, but it does mean that you should give yourself permission to take as much time as you need to work through your loss.

In His Comfort,

The Third Letter

THE TRUTH ABOUT GRIEF

"There is a time for everything, and a season for every activity under heaven: a time to be born and a time to die... a time to weep and a time to laugh, a time to mourn and a time to dance."

Ecclesiastes 3:1,2,4

THE TRUTH ABOUT GRIEF

Dear Peter:

By now you undoubtedly know more about grief than you ever wanted to know. You don't necessarily understand it, but you've experienced it. You know about the desolation of a hauntingly empty house which, not so long ago, resounded to the joyous laughter of your beloved.

You know about eating alone at the table in the sunlit breakfast nook where the two of you so often enjoyed the quiet of early morning and talked of growing old together. You are painfully reminded of your aloneness and your loss each time something — a few bars of a favorite song, a phone call from a friend, an old snapshot — reminds

25

you of a shared experience. Only now you have no one to share your feelings with.

Following the death of his beloved wife Davy, Sheldon Vanauken wrote, "Along with the emptiness, which is what I mean by loss, and along with the grief — loss and grief are not the same thing — *I kept wanting to tell her about it.* We always told each other — that was what sharing was — and now this huge thing was happening to me, and I couldn't tell her...I sometimes thought I could bear the loss and grief if only I could tell her about it."[1] (emphasis mine)

I remember another grieving widower telling me that the hardest thing for him to bear was when something interesting or funny happened and he would think, "I must remember to tell this to Margaret." Then he would be reminded that Margaret was dead. At such times his grief was nearly unbearable.

Because grief is so painful, you have probably been tempted to seek not only relief, but escape. Don't! While that reaction is not unusual, it is counterproductive. As painful as your grief is, it is not a foe to be overcome, but a friend to be embraced. If you insist on thinking of your grief as an enemy, you will only delay the healing process. You may deny your grief, even repress it for a time, but you cannot escape it. One way or the other, you will grieve! The only real choice you have is how and when.

Grief itself is painful, but not injurious. It is a wound that brings healing in much the same way that a proper surgical procedure wounds the body in order to heal it. As C.S. Lewis wrote in a letter to a dear friend whose wife had died: "...I am sure it is never sadness — a proper, straight natural response to loss — that does people harm, but all the other things, all the resentment, dismay, doubt and self-pity with which it is usually complicated."[2]

In the final analysis, Peter, grief is a healing gift from God. Jesus said, "Blessed are those who mourn, for they will be comforted" (Matthew 5:4). That promise is fulfilled when you grieve. When you weep, God weeps with you as surely as Jesus wept with Mary following the death of her brother Lazarus. And as you share your sorrow with God, you will experience His comfort; He will bear a portion of your grief. As the prophet wrote so long ago:

> *Surely he took up our infirmities and* **carried our sorrows**.
>
> Isaiah 53:4

There are those who teach that Christians should not grieve. They reason, falsely, that since our loved ones have gone to be with the Lord, we should rejoice and not weep. Don't be misled, Peter. The Scriptures teach you otherwise. The Apostle Paul tells us in Romans 12:15:

> *Rejoice with those who rejoice; mourn with those who mourn.*

And the writer of Ecclesiastes declares:

> *There is a time for everything, and a season for every activity under heaven...a time to weep and a time to laugh, a time to mourn and a time to dance.*
>
> Ecclesiastes 3:1,4

Peter, now is the time for you to mourn.

Paul, the foremost apologist for the resurrection, affirms both the promise of eternal life, which gives us hope in the dark hour of our loss, and the reality of death, which makes grief mandatory. In his first letter to the believers in Thessalonica he encourages them to grieve, but not in the same way that the world grieves.

He writes:

> *Brothers, we do not want you to be ignorant about those who fall asleep, or to grieve like the rest of men, who have no hope. We believe that Jesus died and rose again and so we believe that God will bring with Jesus those who have fallen asleep in him....*
>
> *He died for us so that, whether we are awake or asleep, we may live together with him.*
>
> 1 Thessalonians 4:13,14; 5:10

Peter, without God death is an unequivocal tragedy; but seen in the light of our Lord's resurrection, it is reduced to a wound to the living. Of course, this knowledge does not eliminate your pain and loss, but it does put it into perspective. You still grieve, but not with the disconsolate grief of those who have no hope of life beyond this world.

As I write these words I can almost see you nodding, as if you want to reassure me, but with a pained and faraway look in your eyes. It's the same look I've seen from time to time as you've hinted at a crises of faith. You've never quite put it into words, but I believe I have sensed it.

If I'm reading something into your words that isn't there, please forgive me. On the other hand, if indeed you are experiencing dark times, times when your sorrow is so deep you find yourself questioning the very existence of God (or at least His goodness), then I want to encourage you. And, if possible, I would like to walk with you through your "dark night of the soul."

You are not the first person who has found himself or herself doubting the very things which they once held most sacred and dear. In fact, such doubt is almost inevitably a part of great grief. That doesn't make your desolation any less painful, but hopefully it does make it less frightening. Sometimes just knowing someone else has gone this way before can be enormously encouraging, especially if you know he or she made it through the ordeal successfully.

I was helped in my own journey by a little book entitled *Tracks of a Fellow Struggler.* It was written by a Baptist minister named John Claypool. It details his personal battle with unbelief as he walked through "the valley of the shadow of death" with his ten-year-old daughter who was fighting a losing battle with leukemia. Just like all grieving persons, he fought a battle of his own, a battle which he describes with moving candor:

"I perhaps need to confess to you that at times in the last few months I have been tempted to conclude that our whole existence is utterly absurd. More than once I looked radical doubt full in the face and honestly wondered if all our talk about love and purpose and a fatherly God were not simply a veil of fantasy that we pathetic humans had projected against the void....

"There were the times, for example, when Laura Lue was hurting so intensely that she had to bite on a rag and used to beg me to pray to God to take away that awful pain. I would kneel down beside her bed and pray with all the faith and conviction of my soul, and nothing would happen except the pain continuing to rage on.

"Or again, that same negative conclusion tempted when she asked me in the dark of the night: 'When will this leukemia go away?' I answered: 'I don't know, darling, but we are doing everything we know to make that happen.' Then she said: 'Have you asked God when it will go away?' And I said: 'Yes, you have heard me pray to Him many times.' But she persisted: 'What did He say? When did He say it would go away?' And I had to admit to myself He had not said a word! I had done a lot of talking and praying and pleading, but the response of the heavens had been silence."[3]

In moments like that, Claypool was tempted to conclude that God, if He existed at all, was either cruel or incompetent. But he resisted that temptation; instead, he clung tenaciously to the conviction that God was good and merciful, even though the pain of his present circumstance seemed to indicate otherwise. By an act of his will he chose to believe that there is more to life than meets the eye. Like Paul, he came to grips with the fact that, "For now we see through a glass, darkly..." (1 Corinthians 13:12 KJV).

Not infrequently we feel ashamed of our grief, especially when we feel angry at God. Somewhere we have picked up the mistaken idea that such feelings reveal something negative about our faith. Nothing could be further from the truth. Peter, the intensity of your grief does not indict your faith; rather, it testifies to the depth of your love and the richness of the relationship you enjoyed with your beloved.

In another sense, the honest acknowledgment of your most real feelings may very well say something about the quality of your faith. Not something negative either, but something positive! It takes tremendous trust to bare your heart and soul to God when to do so requires you to express disappointment, doubt, even anger. Somewhere we have picked up the idea that these are not the kinds of emotions a "true" Christian should have. Still, for the grieving person such feelings are real, and in order to work through them, he must honestly share them with God. It's his only hope. Denial is nothing more than a slow death.

My words may seem blasphemous, as if I am tempting you to commit a sacrilege, but that is not so. God already knows what is in your heart, so what is to be gained by pretending? There is a certain risk, to be sure, when you express your doubts and unbelief, not to mention your anger; after all, you might get "stuck" there. Still, it is the only way. You must trust God to help you work through your feelings.

I am encouraged when I remember that in the hour of His death Jesus experienced the same kind of haunting questions which torment us, yet without being guilty of sin. (Hebrews 4:15.) He too felt that God had forsaken Him: "And at the ninth hour Jesus cried out in a loud voice, *'Eloi, Eloi, lama sabachthani?'* — which means, 'My God, my God, why have you forsaken me?'" (Mark 15:34).

But He did not allow Himself to become trapped there. Having honestly expressed His soul's deepest despair, He was able to move from that tormenting question to an affirmation of His faith:

> *"Father, into your hands I commit my spirit."*
> *When he had said this, he breathed his last.*

> Luke 23:46

Although His circumstances were obviously different from yours, I think there is a truth to be learned. You cannot get beyond your doubts and fears until you honestly face them in God's presence. Having done that, you are free to reaffirm your faith and recommit yourself to the God of all grace!

Of course, that doesn't mean that you are finished with your grief — but that's a letter for another day. It does, however, signal progress. You have moved into a new dimension, a new honesty, in your relationship with God. Now you can walk through "the valley of the shadow of death," not without pain, but without despair, for you do not walk alone, isolated by your stubborn denial.

In His Comfort,

The Fourth Letter

THE TIDES OF GRIEF

"*Praise be to the God and Father of our Lord Jesus Christ, the Father of compassion and the God of all comfort, who comforts us in all our troubles....*"

2 Corinthians 1:3,4

THE TIDES OF GRIEF

Dear Peter:

In your last letter you said that just about the time you thought things were starting to get back to "normal," you were suddenly overwhelmed with a fresh wave of grief. You went on to say that when that happened you felt your loss as acutely as in the days immediately following the funeral. Then you asked, "When will this terrible pain end?"

I wish I knew, but I don't. As I mentioned in an earlier letter, grieving is a lengthy process and often requires two or three years to complete its healing work. Of course, you will not always grieve with the same intensity; no one could bear that. Gradually, you will find that the awful edge of your grief is lessening. You will experience a

39

renewed interest in life. It won't happen all at once, and there will be numerous reversals when you are caught once again in the painful throes of grief. Still, as the seasons pass, you will experience a springtime in your own life as the long winter of your grief draws to a close. One of the best ways to understand what is happening is found in the analogy you used — "a fresh wave of grief."

In truth, grieving is a lot like the tide; it comes in waves. Immediately following the death of a loved one, we are overwhelmed by a sense of loss and accompanying sadness. The tide of grief comes rushing in, but we are protected from the enormity of our loss by shock, by the all-consuming details surrounding the death and burial, and by the comforting presence of family and friends. However, once the funeral is over and life returns to its familiar routine, we experience a great weariness and an unspeakable sadness.

Although this is an overwhelmingly difficult time, it is not unexpected. You were prepared for it; that is, insofar as anyone can be prepared for something never before

40

experienced. With determination you suffered through those first few weeks. There were moments of rage, moments when the injustice of it all incensed you, and you were tempted to blame God. At other times you were unbearably sad. There were even periods of depression when you were tempted to isolate yourself. Still, little by little, the awful edge of your grief dulled. You still hurt, but it was less a searing pain and more a stubborn ache.

Then came the day, at last, when you seemed to awaken from the long night of your grief. It would be going too far to say that you were happy, but at least you were not unhappy, not sad.

For the first time since that fateful moment when you learned of her death, you felt like your old self. (Remember, you called just to tell me how good you were feeling.) You concluded, incorrectly, that you were over your grief. In truth, what you were experiencing that day is similar to what a sick person feels when he finally turns the corner following a lengthy illness. The sky suddenly seems bluer, the sun brighter, and a zest for living returns, but there will still be many days of recuperation before he is fully recovered.

In *A Grief Observed*, C. S. Lewis says, "There are moments, most unexpectedly, when something inside me tries to assure me that I don't really mind so much, not so very much, after all. Love is not the whole of a man's life. I was happy before I ever met H. I've plenty of what are called 'resources.' People get over these things. Come, I shan't do so badly....*Then comes a sudden jab of red-hot memory and all this 'commonsense' vanishes like an ant in the mount of a furnace.*"[1] (emphasis mine)

That, I believe, pretty well sums up what is happening to you now. Following a brief period when you seemed relatively free of grief, you are suddenly finding yourself grieving again. To use your analogy, when you finally thought you were beginning to regain your emotional equilibrium, you were "blind-sided" by a fresh wave of grief.

Now once again you find yourself weeping at the oddest moments. Your melancholy has returned and you've lost all interest in life. People weary you, and yet you can't bear the thought of being alone. You find it hard to follow or respond to their casual conversation; it seems so uninteresting. Yet you want people around, if only they would talk to each other and not you.

This is a pattern which will repeat itself again and again over the next several months. The tides of grief will come in and go out. You will experience times of intense grief followed by periods of relative calm. Then the tide will come in again, and once again you will grieve. Just as suddenly, the tide will go out again so that, if you did not know better, you would think you were finally over your grief. Of course, you're not. This is just another "resting period" before you resume your "grief work."

As grief does its healing work, you will begin to notice some subtle changes. When the tide of grief rolls in, it will not come in quite as far, nor will it stay as long. And when it rolls back, it will go out further and stay out longer. Your times of grief will become briefer and less intense,

43

while your times of rest will become longer and more renewing.

Another subtle change is in the way you think about your beloved. In the initial stages of grief, almost all of your thoughts are filled with loss. As you well know, you cannot think of your beloved without remembering her terrible suffering and the depressing details of her death. The funeral service and the trip to the cemetery are still haunting memories. You brood about what might have been, what should have been. No memory of her is free from pain.

By and by those painful memories will be replaced by earlier ones when you shared the joy of life, reminiscences of happier times when death seemed nothing more than a distant possibility.

The first few times that you remember her without experiencing grief's familiar pangs you will undoubtedly feel guilty, as if you have betrayed her memory. You may find it helpful to remember that as it is unhealthy to repress grief when you experience it, even so it is also unhealthy to manufacture sorrow when it is not there. The healthy griever accepts his feelings as valid, whether sorrow or comfort, and offers them to God in worship.

Another reason you may long to hold onto your sorrow is because it may seem to be all you have left of the life you shared together. In *Song for Sarah* a grieving mother says, "...my feelings are the only thing I have left which haven't been wrested from me. My tears and my pain over you are all I still have which belong to the three of us. Everything else is gone. So even if it does hurt, it's the last thing I have which is ours. Everything else in my life is new — you can see that. These tears are all that's left of us."[2]

In truth, the redemptive work of grief is intended to heal your broken heart so you can remember your beloved without always reliving the pain of her death. Her death may have been the last thing you shared, but it is not the only thing. You also shared her life, and I encourage you to allow the God of all comfort to balance those last painful memories with the early joyous ones. I am not suggesting that you attempt to block out the memory of her death, but only that you make it a part of the integrated whole. As difficult as it may be, you must remember the life she lived as well as the death she died.

In His Comfort,

The Fifth Letter

THE PITFALLS OF GRIEF

"When you pass through the waters, I will be with you; and when you pass through the rivers, they will not sweep over you. When you walk through the fire, you will not be burned; the flames will not set you ablaze. "For I am the Lord, your God, the Holy One of Israel, your Savior...."

Isaiah 43:2,3

THE PITFALLS OF GRIEF

Dear Peter:

As you well know, grief is an inevitable part of our human condition. Sooner or later all of us experience the death of someone we love, and with it the pain of grief. Yet for all of grief's familiarity, few of us are ever prepared for it. As a consequence, we risk not only our future happiness, but our emotional wholeness as well.

During the grieving process you must always avoid two temptations, either of which can be emotionally crippling. The first is the temptation to pretend that you are fully recovered when you are not. As you have undoubtedly discovered, most people are uncomfortable with grief. As long as you are visibly grieving, they may avoid you if they can. Since all of us need acceptance, especially in times of grief and loss, it is natural to hide your grief in order to be accepted. This may seem to work for a time, but in actuality it only delays the healing process.

The rejection you may be experiencing is not personal, although it undoubtedly feels very personal. It is only a reaction common to all who have experienced great grief. For instance, following his wife's death, C. S. Lewis wrote: "An odd by-product of my loss is that I'm aware of being an embarrassment to everyone I meet. At work, at the club, in the street, I see people, as they approach me, trying to make up their minds whether they'll 'say some-thing about it' or not....Some funk [sic] it altogether. R. has been avoiding me for a week."[1] Lewis concludes, somewhat tongue-in-cheek I think, "Perhaps the bereaved ought to be isolated in special settlements like lepers."[2]

Most people who seem to avoid you probably do so because they simply don't know what to say. Nor do they understand the comfort a compassionate listener affords the grieving person. The naked reality of our loss and the intense emotions it has birthed are likely frightening to them. The questions you raise, the pain you share, may well strike too close to home and threaten their carefully constructed world view. Most people are simply not ready — or able — to deal with their own doubts, let alone yours. Whatever the reason, you must never allow their negative reactions to cause you to repress your honest grief in order to avoid rejection.

The second temptation is to wallow in your grief. I'm not suggesting that you deny the reality of your loss in order to appear recovered, but I know that grief has a fatal fascination for most of us. There is something "tragic," even "romantic," about one who has suffered a great loss, especially if he or she seems to suffer nobly. If we are not careful, "bearing our grief" can become a pseudo badge of courage, the thing that sets us apart from all others. After a time it is easier to play the part of the grieving spouse or parent or child than it is to come to grips with our loss and get on with the business of living.

The most common way in which this second temptation manifests itself is through an abnormal and very unhealthy preoccupation with grief. While it is normal to be consumed with "our loss" in the initial stages of grief, past a certain point it becomes counterproductive. Healthy grief may require several months (even as much as two years or more) to complete its work, but it is not static. It moves from a sense of loss to one of grateful appreciation. That is to say, as grief does its healing work, the way we think about the departed will change.

Initially, all we can remember is their sickness and death, but after a while we begin to recall the life we shared together. This change doesn't come about all at once, nor is it final. Little by little we find ourselves remembering the good times we shared together. These positive memories will be interspersed with painful episodes when the memory of their death returns with frightening clarity. Still, as time goes on, more and more of our thoughts will be of the life they lived rather than the death they died. That's the healing power of grief.

Although grief's work cannot be hurried, there are certain things we can do to facilitate it. Let me illustrate.

Some years ago I was working with a mother who was mourning the accidental death of her sixteen-year-old son. When she came to see me, several months had passed, but the full impact of his death was just beginning to sink in. With great sorrow she told me of the funeral and the trip to the cemetery. The day had been cold and rainy and she said it had broken her heart to leave her "little boy" alone in that kind of weather. In fact, she had returned to the cemetery that night, where she had stood at his grave for more than an hour, oblivious to the inclement weather. Having told me that, she hastened to assure me that she knew her son wasn't really in that casket, that his spirit was with God Who gave it, but....

There, in my presence, she began to come to grips with the terrible truth of her son's death. For the first time she dared to put her true feeling into words. Finally, she felt safe enough to give vent to all the grief she had carefully concealed. All she could think about was what he had missed. He never had a date, or owned his own car. He never graduated from high school, never went to his senior prom. He never attended college, or married, or had children of his own. Her list was endless, and in great sorrow she poured out the agony of her soul.

After several sessions, I felt that the time had come for us to move on, so I gently suggested that she spend some time each day remembering the good times she had shared with her son. In order to make the memories specific, I asked her to put them in the form of a letter to her departed son. Finally, I asked her to conclude each letter with a prayer.

My purpose was really very simple. By asking her to recall the good times they had shared, I was encouraging her to recall not just her son's death, but his life as well. Of course, this did not nullify his tragic death, but it did serve to put it into the context of the life he had lived. As long as she had those special memories, her son would never be far from her thoughts. And, by requesting she conclude every letter with a prayer, I was making a way for her to give to God both her grief and her gratitude.

A few days later she wrote:

"Dear Son,

"Today is such a beautiful day. The sun is shining and the leaves are blowing under the trees.

"Remember when we went to the Elephant Rock State Park? You climbed on the big rocks and said, 'Look Mom, I am king of the mountain.' When it was time to go I said, 'Come on Froggie,' and the boys next to you said, 'Froggie? What a funny name for a kid.' We laughed all the way home.

"You were four years old then and I guess that was the day you got your nickname. You never seemed to mind that I called you 'Froggie' all these years. I love you very much.

"Always,

Mom"

She concluded with a prayer:

"Dear God!

"Thank You for the sun and the trees. Thank You for the laughter that only children can bring in their special way.

55

Please Lord, heal my heart and spirit so I can be a light for You."

As the weeks went by, she began to recover. Little by little her good days began to outnumber her bad days. Eventually her memories of her beloved son become a source of comfort rather than searing pangs of grief.

Now when she thinks of him, her first thoughts are usually of some childhood prank, or of some tender, poignant moment, rather than of his fatal accident. Of course, there will always be those times — his birthday or the anniversary of his death — when she will experience again the pain of her loss. But for the most part she is now able to thank God for the sixteen years she and her son had together, rather than blaming Him for his premature death.

Peter, I shared all of this with you because it may be time for you to take control of your grief. For the most part it has been controlling you these past few months — and that's okay. But if you hope to get beyond this point, you will have to take some responsibility for your own recovery.

Maybe the time has come for you to change your focus. Heretofore you have mourned your loss. Perhaps now it is time for you to give thanks for the years you and your beloved had together, thanks for the richness of the life you shared.

In an earlier letter I referred to a little book entitled *Tracks of a Fellow Struggler,* where John Claypool discusses his struggle to make some sense out of the death of his ten-year-old daughter. He concludes: "I have two alternatives: dwelling on the fact that she has been taken away, I can dissolve in remorse that all of this is gone forever; or, focusing on the wonder that she was given to us at all, I can learn to be grateful that we shared life, even for an all-too-short ten years....The way of remorse does not alter the stark reality one whit and only makes matters worse. The way of gratitude does not alleviate the pain, but it somehow puts some light around the darkness and builds strength to begin to move on."[3]

Peter, your beloved was a gift from God, pure and simple. She was never really yours, not in the sense that we tend to think. You were privileged to enjoy life with her for a time...and now she is gone. You can hold that fact against God and grow bitter, or you can thank God that you were given the gift of her presence for a time, however short.

If you choose to thank God for what you have had, rather than to mourn what you have lost, I believe you will discover a new dimension of life. That doesn't mean that you won't grieve, or that you won't miss her. Rather, it means that not even death can rob you of the joys you shared together! Nor can it steal the hope of the presence or the promise of the future. The God Who makes all things new is now present to renew your life. He wants to give you the grace to enjoy living again!

In His Comfort,

The Sixth Letter

THE PROMISE OF HIS PRESENCE

"I took you from the ends of the earth,
from its farthest corners I called you...I have chosen
you and have not rejected you. So do not fear,
for I am with you; do not be dismayed, for I am your
God. I will strengthen you and help you...For I am
the Lord, your God, who takes hold of your right
hand and says to you, Do not fear; I will help you."

Isaiah 41:9,10,13

THE PROMISE OF HIS PRESENCE

Dear Peter:

As a pastor for nearly twenty-five years, I have had many opportunities to share the grief of those whom the Lord has entrusted to my care. Although that has been a tragically sad responsibility at times, it has also afforded me the opportunity to witness not only the faithfulness of God, but also the faith of His people and the strength it provides, especially in the hour of our greatest loss.

Not even those who have great faith, however, endure grief without questions. Inevitably their concerns have a common theme. Although each person expresses his apprehension in his own unique way, it can generally be summed up in two or three common questions.

First, the bereaved want to know if God has forsaken

them, if He has abandoned them in the dark hour of their grief. The emptiness they experience, the desolation they feel, often makes it seem that He has. Second, they want to be assured that God knows what they are experiencing and that He cares. Finally, they ask, "Can God make something good out of this terrible experience?"

As you well know, Peter, one of the things that makes the death of a loved one so difficult is that we often feel that God has forsaken us. Of course, He hasn't, but there are times when it feels as if He has. Such feelings are common to those who are bereaved, and there is no reason to be ashamed of them.

C. S. Lewis, the great Christian apologist, struggled with feelings of abandonment following his wife's death. Of that experience he wrote: "Meanwhile, where is God? This is one of the most disquieting symptoms. When you are happy, so happy that you have no sense of needing Him, so happy that you are tempted to feel His claims upon you as an interruption, if you remember yourself and turn to Him with gratitude and praise, you will be — or so it feels — welcomed with open arms. But go to Him when your need is desperate, when all other help is vain, and what do you find? A door slammed in your face, and a sound of bolting and double bolting on the inside. After that, silence. You may as well turn away. The longer you wait, the more emphatic the silence will become. There are no lights in the windows. It might be an empty house. Was it ever inhabited? It seemed so once. And that seeming was as strong as this. What can this mean? Why is He so present a commander in our time of prosperity and so very absent a help in time of trouble?"[1]

In times like that, we must remember that while our feelings are "real," they are not necessarily accurate. That is to say, it truly feels as if God has deserted us, that He has left us alone with our grief. He hasn't, but it feels as though He has. Through the centuries, spiritual pilgrims have referred to this sense of abandonment as "the dark night of the soul." They triumphed in those dark times by choosing to trust in the truth of God's Word rather than the raging of their emotions.

The Scriptures contain many promises of His abiding presence. Promises like Deuteronomy 31:8 which declares, "The Lord himself goes before you and *will be with you; he will never leave you nor forsake you.* Do not be afraid; do not be discouraged."

The last thing Jesus did before ascending into heaven was to give His disciples the promise of His presence. "...And surely I am with you always, to the very end of the age" (Matthew 28:20).

These promises and countless others like them are a source of tremendous strength when you are grieving. Yet, what has helped me the most in my hour of desolation is a passage from Isaiah 49:

> *...For the Lord comforts his people and will have compassion on his afflicted ones.*
>
> *But Zion said, "The Lord has forsaken me, the Lord has forgotten me."*
>
> *"Can a mother forget the baby at her breast and have no compassion on the child she has*

borne? Though she may forget, I will not forget you!

"See, I have engraved you on the palms of my hands...."

Verses 13-16

Can a mother forget the child she has conceived? Can she forget that joyous moment when she first felt him move within her womb? Can she forget the hours she spent praying and dreaming about their life together? Can she forget the moment of birth, when she went to the very gates of death to bring forth life, when at last the awful agony of labor was forgotten in the delirious joy of holding her tiny child for the very first time?

Can she forget the infant who nursed at her breast? Can she forget?

I cannot imagine how she could, but God says, "...Though she may forget, *I will not forget you!*"

In other words, the only thing worthy to be compared with God's love for us is a mother's love for her child.

Yet, even that special love pales in comparison with God's eternal and unconditional love for His children. As unimaginable as it may seem, there are mothers who abandon their own children, but God will never forsake one of His own!

In the hour of grief — no, I should say in the weeks and months of grief — when it seems there will never be an end to our grieving, when it seems all of life is one sad song, we still have a choice. We can choose to believe what seems to be the truth — God is absent. Or we can ignore the visible evidence in favor of the invisible reality. We can choose to believe that God is present and one day soon our concussive emotions will once again recognize His nearness.

Not infrequently the pain of our loss blinds us to the reality of God's presence. Only later when we look back and review the days of our grief do we realize that He has been with us all the time, even when we were sure that He was nowhere to be found. As Henri Nouwen points out in The Genesee Diary, "What is most close, most intimate, most present, often cannot be experienced directly but only with a certain distance.... Only in retrospect do I realize that something very important has taken place. Isn't this true of all the really important events of life? When I am together with someone I love very much, we seldom talk about our relationship. The relationship, in fact, is too central to be a subject of talk. But later after we have separated and write letters, we realize how much it all meant to us, and we even write about it."[2]

Isn't this what happened to the grieving disciples on the road to Emmaus? Jesus spent an entire day with them, even expounded the Scriptures to them, and yet they did not recognize Him. Only later, when He had disappeared from their sight, did they begin to reflect on their experience. Then they said, "...'Were not our hearts burning within us while he talked with us on the road and opened the Scriptures to us?'" (Luke 24:32).

At other times God manifests His presence indirectly, through other people. Paul writes, "...when we came into Macedonia, this body of ours had no rest, but we were harassed at every turn — conflicts on the outside, fears within. But God, who comforts the downcast, comforted us by the coming of Titus..." (2 Corinthians 7:5,6).

Remember the lady I wrote about whose teenaged son died in a tragic accident? One morning when she was feeling particularly low (or to use her words, "really in the pits"), her doorbell rang. She wrestled momentarily with the idea of ignoring it. Her eyes were red from crying, her hair was a mess and she was still in her robe. It rang again, and she forced herself toward the front door.

The caller was a friend from church, and when Joyce opened the door, she breezed right in announcing, "I've come to talk with you." Noticing Joyce's disheveled appearance, she quickly added, "And if you don't feel like talking, I'll just sit with you, and if you want to cry," she continued, brandishing a box of tissue, "I'm prepared to cry with you."

By this time they were back in the kitchen where the uninvited guest proceeded to rummage around until she found the coffeemaker and got it going. The two friends spent the rest of the morning over coffee, which was laced with conversation and tears. As they talked, the strangest thing happened — Joyce began to feel better. She was still sad, but now she was no longer alone with her sadness. A friend was present and shared her sorrow. And in some mysterious way God was present, too, and He comforted her.

When Joyce related that incident to me, she concluded very wistfully, "If only there were more people like her. And she brought her own tissue! Can you believe that?"

Think for a moment, Peter. How many times over these past weeks and months has someone been there for you? Oh, I know the many times we have failed you: the long evenings you've spent alone, the meals taken by yourself, the telephone that never rang. Still, think of the times you have been comforted in your grief by a phone call at just the "right time." Coincidence? Hardly. And what about the cards and letters, the notes that seemed to come with an inspiring word just when you were on the verge of giving up. Coincidence? Hardly.

Maybe Alexander Irvine expressed it best in his novel *My Lady of the Chimney Corner*. Irvine has "the lady" go comfort a neighbor whose boy lay dead:

"As gently as falls an autumn leaf, she laid her hand on Eliza's head: 'Ah, woman, God isn't a printed book to be carried aroun' by a man in fine clothes, not a cross danglin' at the watch chain of a priest. God takes a hand whenever He can find it and does what He likes with it. Sometimes He takes a Bishop's hand and lays it on a child's head in benediction, and then He takes the hand of a doctor to relieve pain, the hand of a mother to guide a child, and sometimes He takes the hand of a poor old craither like me to give comfort to a neighbor. But they're all hands touched by His Spirit, and His Spirit is everywhere lukin' for hands to use."[3]

Remember Peter, the hand that brings you comfort and encouragement is always God's hand, and He is never far from His own.

In His Comfort,

The Seventh Letter

THE DEPTH OF HIS LOVE

"'I have told you these things,
so that in me you may have peace.
In this world you will have trouble.
But take heart!
I have overcome the world.'"

John 16:33

THE DEPTH OF HIS LOVE

Dear Peter:

Again and again, these past weeks you have asked, "Does God know what's happening to me? Does He care?" At other times you have wondered, "Why didn't He do something to prevent this awful tragedy?"

I've given considerable thought to your questions, and I am convinced that it's not really answers you seek as much as assurance. Intuitively you know that suffering and death are often shrouded in mystery, that there are simply no pat answers. Still, the nagging questions remain, replayed in your mind, over and over again. You long for some word, some explanation, which will restore your confidence. As it is, you are beset by a haunting uncertainty. Although you may never have put it into words, I sense that deep down you wonder if you can really trust God.

Don't be embarrassed: your doubts are as old as mankind. In the midst of grief almost everyone is tempted to feel the way you do. Yet, at the same time you love God more intensely than you ever have. These feelings may seem contradictory to you, and you may even be tempted to wonder if you are losing your mind. You're not! Grief gives birth to a host of different emotions. The Lord understands this, and He comes to us in the midst of our emotional storms.

Following the unexpected death of their brother, Lazarus, Martha and Mary experienced an overwhelming grief which gave birth to questions not unlike your own. Like you, they were troubled by the tragedy of losing a loved one and they could not help but question our Lord's goodness.

"'Lord,' Martha said to Jesus, 'if you had been here, my brother would not have died'" (John 11:21). With those emotional words she accused Jesus of failing, of not caring, or ignoring them in the hour of their greatest need. (Does that sound familiar?)

What did Jesus do? How did He respond? He absorbed her anger without rebuke. He understood how things must seem from her limited perspective, how much she loved her brother, and how deeply she hurt.

Yet, she didn't stop there. Like you, she still loved Jesus intensely and wanted to believe. Even in her anger, her faith expressed itself: "'...I know he will rise again in the resurrection at the last day...I believe that you are the Christ, the Son of God, who was to come into the world'" (John 11:24,27).

When she quickly moved from anger to faith, Jesus met her there and built on her confession. He said to her, "...'I am the resurrection and the life. He who believes in me will live, even though he dies; and whoever lives and believes in me will never die. Do you believe this?'" (John 11:25). And Martha answered, "Yes, Lord..." (John 11:27).

Mary responded differently. She too was hurt and angry, maybe more hurt and angry in keeping with her temperament.

"When Mary reached the place where Jesus was and saw him, she fell at his feet and said, 'Lord, if you had been here, my brother would not have died.'

"When Jesus saw her weeping...he was deeply moved in spirit and troubled...[and] Jesus wept" (John 11:32, 33,35).

Notice that Jesus also met Mary where she was. And there was little or no faith in her confession, beyond the faith to tell Jesus how she really felt. Somehow, even in her grief and disappointment, she believed He would understand, and He did. For her, He had no theological pronouncements, no revelation about resurrection life, no discourse about His divine Sonship. Why? Not because these things were any less true now, but because Mary was not ready to receive them. There was nothing in her heart but sorrow and tears, so He met her at the place of her grief. He wept with her.

If Jesus came to Martha and Mary in the hour of their grief, will He not come to you? If He understood what they were feeling and shared their feelings, will He not do as much for you? How did I put it in my first letter? "When tragedy strikes, when a loved one dies, God's heart is the first of all hearts to break!"

I'm hesitant, Peter, to give you too many scriptures because I know that the shock of grief can render the eternal Scriptures temporarily unreal. Yet, I also know that nothing comforts and illuminates the Word of God, especially when it is spoken in season. Nothing so quiets the frightened heart, so stills the troubled soul, as the Holy Scriptures.

Think for a moment. Haven't there been times, especially of late, when the Scriptures have spoken to the deepest and most profound longings of your soul? Haven't you discovered new words of hope and encouragement in familiar verses, passages which you've known for years? Is this mere chance? Not on your life! It is God's way of manifesting Himself, His way of comforting you in the depths of your grief.

Your questions may still remain, but somehow they don't seem quite so important now. God has given you something better than understanding — a trust. A trust which is rooted, not in explanation, but in the assurance that He cares.

Dr. David McKenna, president of Asbury Theological Seminary, tells of a friend who lost his daughter in a flash flood along the Thompson River in Colorado. He says, "When I met him two weeks after the tragedy, his eyes were sunk in dark sockets from weeping. Awkwardly, I asked, 'How is it going?'

"Never given to public testimony or eloquent statements, his sad eyes looked back, and he spoke almost from a trance, 'The hurt goes deep, but His love goes deeper.'"[1]

That, Peter, is the essence of trust. No matter how deep your grief, God's love goes deeper still.

In His Comfort,

The Eighth Letter

IF GOD BE FOR US

"And we know that in all things God works for the good of those who love him, who have been called according to his purpose....

"What, then, shall we say in response to this? If God is for us, who can be against us?"

Romans 8:28,31

The Eighth Letter

IF GOD BE FOR US

Dear Peter:

I couldn't agree with you more when you say that one of the things that makes death so difficult to accept is that it seems such a waste. As rational creatures, we find simply unbearable the thought that a fatal accident or illness might be pointless, of no eternal value. On the other hand, if we can be assured God will ultimately bring good out of what looks for all the world like a senseless tragedy, then we can somehow endure it.

Given that hope, it is not uncommon for the bereaved to try to figure out how God is going to bring good out of their tragedy. It is a futile exercise, for the most part, because God's ways are far beyond anything we could ever imagine. In fact, trying to discover His ultimate purpose in such situations often leads to absurd conclusions or to outright despair.

I am not suggesting, not even for a moment, that God caused the death of your beloved, but for certain He will redeem it, that is, bring eternal good out of even your unspeakable loss. The very thing that the enemy intended to use to destroy your faith can become an instrument by which God furthers His eternal purpose in your life and in the kingdom. Just how He will do that, I don't know; but that He will do so, I am sure.

Many years ago, I heard about a minister whose son committed suicide. Ten days after the funeral, the minister entered the pulpit and announced his text. Under real duress, he read Romans 8:28: "And we know that in all things God works for the good of those who love him, who have been called according to his purpose." Visibly struggling, he said:

"I cannot make my son's suicide fit into this passage. It's impossible for me to see how anything good can come out of it. Yet, I realize that I only see in part; I only know in part. The scope of this verse is beyond me; I can't comprehend it. Still, somehow it supports me, enables me to go on living even though life doesn't seem to make any sense. Somehow I believe that when all of life is over, when God has fully worked out His perfect will, even my son's suicide will be woven into the final tapestry of His eternal design.

"It's like the miracle of the shipyard. Almost every part of our great oceangoing vessels is made of steel. If you take any single part — be it a steel plate out of the hull or the huge rudder — and throw it into the ocean, it will sink. Steel doesn't float! But when the shipbuilders are finished, when the last plate has been riveted in place, when the last part has been bolted properly, then that massive ship is virtually unsinkable. By the design of the master shipbuilder, steel has been made to float!

"Taken by itself, my son's suicide is senseless. Throw it into the sea of Romans 8:28, and it sinks. But I believe that when the Eternal Shipbuilder has finally finished, when God has worked out His perfect design, even this senseless tragedy will somehow work to our eternal good. I can't even imagine how, but I know it will!"

Peter, you asked me what good can possibly come out of your beloved's death. I wish I could tell you, but I can't. All I can do is assure you that God is too wise ever to make a mistake. And He is too loving ever to cause one of His children needless pain.

I see you struggling to make some sense of this tragic death, trying to see how it can possibly be made to fit into your understanding of God's perfect plan. I don't fault you for this, but I must counsel you to be careful. Death is not a riddle to be solved, or a question to be answered; instead, it is a mystery to be entrusted to the wisdom of God.

Rather than trying to understand how God is going to bring good out of your beloved's death, it might be more beneficial to consider some historic examples of how He has redeemed other seemingly senseless tragedies. Not infrequently the good that God works can only be seen in retrospect. Even then we only see in part. We must wait until eternity to understand the full scope of His eternal craftsmanship.

For instance, on January 8, 1956, Jim Elliot and four other missionaries were brutally murdered by the Aucas, a savage tribe of manhunters living in the Ecuadorian jungles. At first glance, their deaths seem like a tragic waste of life, especially Jim Elliot's. Not only was he a young husband and father, he was also a missionary of rare and special ability.

Even as an undergraduate at Wheaton College, he had evidenced a remarkable spiritual maturity. His personal pilgrimage is chronicled in his diary (published posthumously as *The Journal of Jim Elliot*) which contains some of the most profound spiritual concepts recorded this century.

His entire life was characterized by a burning passion to reach the unreached peoples of the world with the Gospel of Jesus Christ. Just prior to his death, he completed a translation of the Gospel of Luke for the Quichuas, a tribe of South American Indians.

In light of all of this, we are tempted to ask why God would allow such a gifted and dedicated young man to be martyred at the age of twenty-nine. His ministry was just beginning. Surely the kingdom could not afford the loss of one so able.

Upon further examination, however, we can see God working to redeem this tragedy: "When news of the death of the five missionaries was announced in Christian schools, hundreds of young people volunteered to take their place. The story caused world missions to be front page news in *Life* magazine and newspapers around the world. Elizabeth Elliot's books about Jim's death, *Through the Gates of Splendor,* and his life, *Shadow of the Almighty,* became missionary classics.

Helen Roseveare, who served for many years in the Belgian Congo as a missionary doctor with the Worldwide Evangelism Crusade, shared a touching incident which further shows how God brings good out of tragedy. She reports:

"A young missionary couple during their first term of

service in a foreign land were expecting their first baby. The mother wrote me from the hospital a few days after the birth to tell me that her baby had died....She went on in her letter, 'Local women whom I've been trying to reach with the gospel visited me yesterday, and their loving sympathy was very touching. Then one of them said to me, "Now you are the same as us. Now we will listen to what you tell us." I find my heart rising above my sorrow...I can identify with the local community in their daily sufferings and so be able to share Christ with them.'"[1]

When Dale Evans Rogers lost her precious two-year-old daughter, Robin, she poured out her grief and her hope in a beautiful book entitled *Angel Unaware*. Because she was willing to be honest and to allow God to use her loss, society's attitude and treatment of mongoloid children was drastically changed.

Dr. Norman Vincent Peale wrote of Dale:

"She is a mother who has won great victory over great sorrow...I saw at once that Robin, her baby, had not lived and died in vain. Where most babies die and leave the mother crushed, Robin put on immortality and her mother found the very joy of God in what might otherwise have been an overwhelming tragedy."[2]

Given these examples and many others like them, one might be tempted to conclude that God caused these deaths in order to advance the work of the Gospel. I cannot believe that. God is not the author of death, but of life.

Death is the archenemy of God, a consequence of humanity's fallen state. It is a defeated enemy, to be sure, but it has not yet been destroyed:

> *For he [Jesus] must reign until he has put all his enemies under his feet. The last enemy to be destroyed is death...*
> *...then the saying that is written will come true: "Death has been swallowed up in victory."*
>
> *"Where, O death, is your victory? Where, O death, is your sting?"*

> *The sting of death is sin...But thanks be to God! He gives us the victory through our Lord Jesus Christ.*
>
> 1 Corinthians 15:25,26,54-57

God uses death in the same way an expert in self-defense uses his opponent's weight and momentum against him. When death strikes, God takes this often unspeakable loss and uses it as an opportunity to bring good out of evil.

Of course, Peter, I must admit that it is much easier for me to write about these truths than it is for you to live them. Although my heart hurts for my suffering, it is nothing compared to your grief. I can view these tragic events somewhat objectively; you cannot. In many ways I am an outside observer, while you are the central figure. As the main participant, you obviously know more about the devastation of death; but as a more objective observer, I probably have a better understanding of the big picture. And in order to make some sense of your loss, you must not insist on seeing it as an entity unique unto itself. You must come to the place where you can view it as a single piece of an integrated whole — a piece which finds its true meaning only in relationship to the eternal whole.

Let me illustrate:

"In June 1815 the English military forces under the Duke of Wellington engaged the forces of Napoleon Bonaparte. All England awaited news of the outcome. It was before the days of fast communication, and watchers were stationed along England's coast to observe the sailing vessels come up the Channel. Any special news would be wigwagged by semaphore to those waiting.

"Knowing the battle was to be fought, the coastal sentries waited for a message of its outcome. Finally, a watcher noted a message being waved from a passing boat, 'Wellington defeated....' And then the fog closed in. The words were relayed across England, and the nation was plunged into gloom.

"When the fog cleared again, another sailor on another boat waved the same message — this time without interruption: 'Wellington defeated the enemy.' England's sorrow was banished and the entire country went wild with joy."[3]

In the befogging pain of our grief, we are able to see only part of the message, and as a result, death often seems like the ultimate insult. It appears to be the final indignity which makes a mockery of our faith. But when the fog of grief begins to clear, even just a little — when at last we are able to perceive the "whole" truth — it becomes obvious that death is a defeated enemy, one which God uses for His eternal purposes until He ultimately destroys it.

> *Therefore we do not lose heart. Though outwardly we are wasting away, yet inwardly we are being renewed day by day.*
>
> *For our light and momentary troubles are achieving for us an eternal glory that far outweighs them all.*
>
> *So we fix our eyes not on what is seen, but on what is unseen. For what is seen is temporary,*

but what is unseen is eternal.

2 Corinthians 4:16-18

Peter, in closing let me say that I am not naive enough to think that anything I write can eliminate the painfulness of your grief. You do not lose someone you love dearly without experiencing the deepest pain of which the human heart is capable. I do believe, however, that the spiritual and emotional devastation caused by your grief can be minimized — no, more than that, redeemed — if you can be helped to see it in its eternal context.

Once you have accomplished that feat, your grief will not necessarily be less, but it will become pain with a purpose. And history has shown us that humans can bear an almost unlimited amount of suffering if they can be assured that it will count for something.

Let me encourage you to offer your beloved's death, along with your grief and loss, as a gift to God. Give Him permission to use it any way He sees fit. Do this, and I truly believe that God will redeem it for His glory and your good.

In His Comfort,

The Ninth Letter

IN MY FATHER'S HOUSE

"'Do not let your hearts be troubled. Trust in God; trust also in me. In my Father's house are many rooms; if it were not so, I would have told you. I am going there to prepare a place for you. And if I go and prepare a place for you, I will come back and take you to be with me that you also may be where I am.'"

John 14:1-3

IN MY FATHER'S HOUSE

Dear Peter:

As I look back over the correspondence we have shared these past months, I am struck by the fact that we have said so little about your beloved. Our letters have focused on what has been happening to you — your grief and your loss.

To an uninitiated observer this might appear very self-centered, even unfeeling, but it is neither. In truth, it is an affirmation of our belief in eternal life. We have never concerned ourselves with Karen's present state because we are confident, as Paul says, that "...to be absent from the body...[is]...to be present with the Lord" (2 Corinthians 5:8 KJV).

95

Having said that, however, I do think the time has come for us to address the question of life after death. This single issue, more than any other, distinguishes the way believers grieve from the way those without the hope of eternal life deal with death.

Until the very moment of death, Peter, all of your thoughts were for your beloved. You agonized as you watched her suffer, tormented by your own inability to do anything to relieve her pain. You seemed to die a little each day as you watched her grow weaker. Yet, when she breathed her last, your awful grief was tempered by the knowledge that she was home at last with the Lord of life. Her suffering was over. Never again would she writhe in pain.

Later when you wrote to thank me for being with you during her last days, you included a few words from a book I had sent you. Do you remember? You quoted from *A Severe Mercy* by Sheldon Vanauken:

"As I stood there in that suddenly empty room, I was suddenly swept with a tide of absolute *knowing*

96

that Davy still was. I do not mean that I thought her body might still live; I knew it didn't. But past faith and belief, I knew quite overwhelmingly that she herself — her soul — still was."[1]

Then you wrote, "Better than anything I might say, this passage describes what happened to me when Karen died. I knew, in a way I had never known anything before, that she was more alive than she had ever been. Even during my darkest hours, when grief made my life nearly unbearable, I never wished to bring her back, not if it meant she would ever have to suffer again. I have to admit though, that I sometimes begged God to take my life. For the first time, I think, I know something of what Paul might have felt when he wrote, '...I desire to depart and be with Christ, which is better by far' (Philippians 1:23)."

When I read those words, Peter, I kept thinking that your confidence in Karen's immortality was well justified. Jesus said, "I am the resurrection and the life. He who believes in me will live, even though he dies" (John 11:25).

Although none of us knows exactly what happens at the moment of death, both Scripture and experience give us every reason to believe that all is well.

When I was a young man in my first pastorate, I had the honor of ministering to a wonderful Christian lady as she faced death. She was suffering from terminal cancer and as she grew physically weaker I could not help but notice how her thoughts turned more and more toward heaven.

As the moment of her death drew near, she fixed her attention on the opposite side of the room, and the most peaceful expression settled on her countenance. Just before she drew her last breath she said, in a voice barely audible, "Jesus. I see Jesus."

Now if this experience were an isolated incident, it would be comforting, but not necessarily conclusive. But it is not an isolated incident. Scripture and experience combine to testify to the fact that there is life after death. Taken together, they constitute an impressive witness and a continuing source of encouragement.

Stephen, the first Christian martyr, cried out as he was being stoned: "'Look,' he said, 'I see heaven open and the Son of Man standing at the right hand of God'" (Acts 7:56).

Ruth Graham, wife of Billy Graham, tells about an experience she had in China. On the station where she lived, one of the evangelistic missionaries was Ad Talbot, whom she affectionately called Uncle Ad. Talbot had five sons and a daughter, Margaret Gay, a girl he deeply loved. Sometime after her death he was in the country with a Chinese Christian woman who was dying. As he knelt beside her bed, the old woman's face lit up and she said to Uncle Ad, "I see heaven, and Jesus is on the right hand of God, and Margaret Gay is with Him." At that moment the room was filled with heavenly music and the Chinese woman was dead.[2]

As you know, Peter, Christianity teaches that at the instant of death, our new life begins. The moment we take our final breath on earth, we take our first breath in heaven. Our bodies are placed in the grave to await the resurrection, but our spirits are immediately present with the Lord.

Dr. George C. Robinson, one-time Professor of Old Testament, McCormick Theological Seminary, once remarked, "Most people dread death, but personally, I am not afraid to die, though I don't court death.... Christians face death with faith, believing that it opens the door 'to a land of goodness and gladness....' Sudden death means sudden glory. Think of the thrill the believer will feel upon arriving home."

"Think of stepping on shore,
And finding it heaven!
Think of taking hold of a hand,
And finding it God's hand!
Think of breathing a new air
And finding it celestial air!
Of feeling invigorated,
And finding it immortality!

Of passing from storm and tempest into
perfect calm!
Of awaking and knowing —
I am home!"[3]

When Karen died, her spirit went immediately to be
with the Lord. Even as you were making the painful
preparations for her funeral, she was fully alive. Yet her
redemption is not complete, and will not be until she
receives her glorified body at the Second Coming of
Christ. Now she eagerly awaits the redemption of her
body. (Romans 8:23.)

Her burial, according to Scripture, was like the planting
of a seed:

> *When you sow, you do not plant the body that
> will be, but just a seed...*
>
> *...The body that is sown is perishable, it is
> raised imperishable;*
>
> *it is sown in dishonor, it is raised in glory; it is
> sown in weakness, it is raised in power;*

101

> *it is sown a natural body, it is raised a
> spiritual body.*
>
> 1 Corinthians 15:37,42-44

The question before us then is not, "Is there life after
death?" That's a scriptural certainty. But rather, "What is
the nature of that life?" What we want to know is, "How
are the dead raised? With what kind of body will they
come?" (1 Corinthians 15:35).

Most of our questions regarding the details of eternal
life will probably go unanswered. The reality of our
immortality is simply beyond us. We have no present
frame of reference, nothing to which we can compare it.
Any earthly thing God might use as a way of comparison
would diminish the glories of heaven at least as much as it
revealed them. As a consequence, most attempts to
describe heaven are little more than exercises in futility.

As you may remember, following Davy's death
Sheldon Vanauken wrote an essay speculating about the
nature of their eternal life together and the activities in
which they might be engaged in the hereafter. In the end

he acknowledged that he had attempted the impossible: "Of course it will not be like that. What it will be is quite beyond anything we can imagine."[4]

Anyone who has ever seriously tried to describe this eternal realm knows something of his frustration. For instance, the Apostle Paul wrote:

> *Fourteen years ago I was taken up to heaven for a visit. Don't ask me whether my body was there or just my spirit, for I don't know; only God can answer that. But anyway, there I was in paradise, and heard things so astounding that they are beyond a man's power to describe or put in words (and anyway I am not allowed to tell them to others).*

> 2 Corinthians 12:2-4 TLB

Given that truth, perhaps the place to start is not with heaven, but with our glorified bodies. If we can come to some understanding of what they will be like, then maybe we can imagine, at least in some small way, the glories of heaven. Since our resurrected bodies will be fashioned after our Lord's glorious body (Philippians 3:21), we need look no further than the risen Christ to see what they will be like.

The first thing one notices about Jesus, following His resurrection, is that His appearance is so "human." Although He has a spiritual body, it is composed of flesh and bone. The disciples could see Him with their natural eyes, and they could touch Him with their natural hands. When He appeared to them following His resurrection, He said, "Look at my hands and my feet. It is I myself! Touch me and see; a ghost does not have flesh and bones, as you see I have" (Luke 24:39).

In fact, His appearance was so "ordinary" that on that first Easter morning Mary Magdalene mistook Him for the gardener. (John 20:10-16.) Then later that same day, two disillusioned disciples journeyed with Him from Jerusalem to Emmaus without even recognizing Him. They thought He was just another weary traveler on the road. (Luke 24:13-35.)

On more than one occasion after His resurrection Jesus enjoyed a meal with His friends. The first time He appeared to His disciples, He asked them, "'Do you have anything here to eat?' They gave him a piece of broiled fish, and he took it and ate it in their presence" (Luke 24:41-43). On another occasion He surprised the disciples by preparing breakfast for them on the beach following a long night of fishing. (John 21:1-14.)

Yet, for all that, Jesus Christ's resurrected body was no ordinary body. He was not limited by time or space. He appeared and disappeared at will, suddenly materializing in the presence of those who believed in Him, and just as suddenly disappearing, only to reappear some place else. In truth, His resurrected body had all the advantages of this natural body, but none of its limitations. And since our mortal bodies will be transformed into the likeness of His glorious body (Philippians 3:21), we too can expect to enjoy the same freedom from the limits of time and space.

I would like to think, Peter, that in heaven we will be able to eat without getting fat; we will be able to exercise without growing sore; that we will be able to work without becoming weary; that we will be able to love without being jealous or possessive; that we will be able to enjoy relationships without misunderstanding; that we will be able to worship fully and uninhibitedly; and that we will be able, finally, to know God completely even as He knows us.

In heaven, singers will sing as they have never sung before. Composers will compose new music and on a scale heretofore unknown. Creative geniuses will continue to invent. Gifted craftsmen will design and build things their natural minds couldn't even conceive. Writers will write, and preachers will preach — only in that glorious realm everything will be done on a scale never imagined by mortal man.

Now look what I've done. I've allowed myself to be drawn into the very trap I was determined to avoid — using earthly comparisons in an attempt to describe heaven's eternal glories. It simply will not work! How did Vanauken put it? "Of course it will not be like that. What it will be is quite beyond anything we can imagine."[5] And so it will:

> *No eye has seen, no ear has heard, no mind*
> *has conceived what God has prepared for those*
> *who love him.*
>
> 1 Corinthians 2:9

Peter, although we cannot conceive of heaven's glories, the promise of eternal life provides an undeniable strength in the time of loss, as well as an unwavering hope for the future. It does not eliminate the pain of our grief, but it does put it into perspective. Let me illustrate.

Some years ago my brother and his family left the United States to become missionaries in Argentina. For them, it was the fulfillment of a lifelong dream. For the rest of us it was a painfully blessed moment. We were happy for Don and his family. He had prepared his entire life for this moment. We knew that He would be happier in Argentina, that this work was what he was destined to do. Still, we were nearly overwhelmed with our grief. All we could think about were the thousands of miles that would separate us, the four years we would be apart. Try as we might, we could not hold back our tears.

With a determined effort we reminded ourselves that this separation, painful though it was, was only temporary. All of us would be reunited in the not-too-distant future. Without question, that was a comfort to us as we said our good-byes, but it did not fill the emptiness we felt as Don and his family boarded that huge 747. Nor did it stop our tears. Yet, even as we cried we were also rejoicing.

That's how believers grieve when a loved one dies. Not without hope and fatalistically (as those who have no assurance of eternal life); but not without tears either, for death creates a great void in the lives of those who are left behind.

For the departed believer, death is not the end of life; rather, it is simply the end of sin, sorrow and suffering. His life (or in the case of Karen, her life) continues, and on a scale heretofore unimagined:

> *And I heard a loud voice from the throne saying, "Now the dwelling of God is with men, and he will live with them. They will be his people, and God himself will be with them and be their God.*
>
> *He will wipe every tear from their eyes. There will be no more death or mourning or crying or pain, for the old order of things has passed away."*
>
> Revelation 21:3,4

Peter, we both know that Karen is with Jesus. She is more alive now than she has ever been. Still, that does not mean that you should not grieve. Yet, even in the midst of your grief, you can find comfort in the promise of an eternal reunion. In eternity you will be reunited with your beloved; you will renew your relationship, and on a higher level than any you ever experienced here.

I say that based on what both Scripture and reason reveal about life after death. Although the ultimate reality of heaven is beyond our comprehension, God has revealed the essence of it. And always that essence is of a far grander scale than anything this earthly life affords. That being the case, how can we doubt that our most intimate earthly relationships will not be somehow enhanced in heaven? I agree with C. S. Lewis who said, "I think the union between the risen spouses will be as close as that between the soul and its own risen body."[6]

Peter, take hope, the best is yet to come!

In His Comfort,

HOW TO RECEIVE JESUS

If you have never received Jesus Christ as your personal Lord and Savior, why not do it right now. Simply repeat this prayer with sincerity:

"Lord Jesus, I believe that You are the Son of God. I believe that You became a man and died on the cross for my sins. I believe that God raised You from the dead and made You the Savior of the world. I confess that I am a sinner and I ask You to forgive me and cleanse me of all of my sins. I accept Your forgiveness and I receive You as my Lord and Savior. In Jesus' name I pray. Amen."

If you confess with your mouth, "Jesus is Lord," and believe in your heart that God raised him from the dead, you will be saved. For it is with your heart that you believe and are justified, and it is with your mouth that you confess and are saved...For everyone who calls on the name of the Lord will be saved.

Romans 10:9,10,13

If we confess our sins, he is faithful and just and will forgive us our sins and purify us from all unrighteousness.

1 John 1:9

Chapter 2

[1]Joe Bayly, quoted in *Training Christians to Counsel* by H. Norman Wright (Denver: Christian Marriage Enrichment, 1977), p. 133.

Chapter 3

[1]Sheldon Vanauken, *A Severe Mercy* (New York: Harper & Row Publishers, 1977), pp. 180,181.

[2]C. S. Lewis, quoted in *A Severe Mercy* by Sheldon Vanauken (New York: Harper & Row Publishers, 1977), p. 183.

[3]John Claypool, *Tracks of a Fellow Struggler* (Waco: Word Books, 1974), p. 77.

Chapter 4

[1]C. S. Lewis, *A Grief Observed* (New York: The Seabury Press, A Crossroad Book, 1961), pp. 7,8.

[2]Paula D'Arcy, *Song for Sarah* (Wheaton, IL: Harold Shaw Publishers, 1979), p. 76.

Chapter 5

[1] C. S. Lewis, *A Grief Observed* (New York: The Seabury Press, A Crossroad Book, 1961), p. 12.

[2] Ibid., p. 13.

[3] John Claypool, *Tracks of a Fellow Struggler* (Waco: Word Books, 1974), pp. 82,83.

Chapter 6

[1] C. S. Lewis, *A Grief Observed* (New York: The Seabury Press, A Crossroad Book, 1961), p. 9.

[2] Henri J. Nouwen, quoted in *Disciplines for the Inner Life* by Bob Benson and Michael W. Benson (Waco: Word Books, 1985), p. 189.

[3] Alexander Irvine, *My Lady of the Chimney Corner*, quoted in Barefoot Days of the Soul, by Maxie Dunnam (Waco: Word Books Publishers, 1969), pp. 114,115.

Chapter 7

[1] David McKenna, *The Jesus Model* (Waco: Word Books Publisher, 1977), p. 41.

Chapter 8

[1]Helen Roseveare, "The Spirit's Enablement," quoted in *Confessing Christ as Lord: The Urbana '81 Compendium,* edited by John W. Alexander (Downer's Grove, IL: InterVaristy Press, 1982), p. 170.

[2]Dr. Norman Vincent Peale, quoted in *Mourning Song* by Joyce Landorf (Old Tappen: Fleming H. Revell Company, 1974), pp. 156,157.

[3]Richard E. Orchard, "Our Magnificent Hope" (*Advance Magazine*, Vol. 4, No. 4, April 1968), p. 4.

Chapter 9

[1]Sheldon Vanauken, *A Severe Mercy* (New York: Harper & Row Publishers, 1977), p. 176.

[2]Billy Graham, *Facing Death and the Life After* (Waco: Word Books, 1987), pp. 239,240.

[3]Herbert Lockyer, *The Funeral Sourcebook* (Grand Rapids: Zondervan Publishing House, 1967), p. 183.

[4]Vanauken, p. 204.

[5]Ibid.

[6]C. S. Lewis, quoted in *A Severe Mercy* by Sheldon Vanauken, p. 205.

BIBLIOGRAPHY

Alexander, John, Ed. *Confessing Christ as Lord: The Urbana '81 Compendium.* Downer's Grove, IL: InterVaristy Press, 1982.

Benson, Bob and Benson, Michael W. *Disciplines for the Inner Life.* Waco: Word books, 1985.

Claypool, John. *Tracks of a Fellow Struggler.* Waco: Word Books, 1974.

D'Arcy, Paula. *Song for Sarah.* Wheaton, IL: Harold Shaw Publishers, 1979.

Dunnam, Maxie. *Barefoot Days of the Soul.* Waco, TX: Word Book Publisher, 1969.

Elliot, Elizabeth. *Shadow Of The Almighty.* San Francisco, CA: Harper & Row, Publishers, 1958.

Graham, Billy. *Facing Death and the Life After.* Waco: Word Books, 1987.

Landorf, Joyce. *Mourning Song*. Old Tappan: Fleming H. Revell Company, 1974.

Lewis, C. S. *A Grief Observed*. New York: The Seabury Press, A Crossroad Book, 1961.

Lockyer, Herbert. *The Funeral Sourcebook.* Grand Rapids: Zondervan Publishing House, 1967.

McKenna, David. *The Jesus Model.* Waco, TX: Word Books Publisher, 1977.

Orchard, Richard E. "Our Magnificent Hope." *Advance Magazine,* Volume 4, No. 4, April 1968.

Vanauken, Sheldon. *A Severe Mercy*. New York: Harper & Row Publishers, 1977.

Wright, H. Norman. *Training Christians to Counsel*. Denver: Christian Marriage Enrichment, 1977.

Richard Exley draws upon his rich diversity of experience as an author, radio host, and conference and retreat speaker to express the thoughts and feelings most of us have never been able to put into words. Richard lives with his wife Brenda in a cabin on Beaver Lake in the Ozarks, and has authored many life-changing books, among them:

Blue-Collar Christianity
Perils of Power
The Rhythm of Life
The Other God— Seeing God As He Really Is
Building Relationships That Last — Life's Bottom Line
Straight From the Heart for Dad (Mom, Graduates, Couples)
How to Be a Man of Character In a World of Compromise
Marriage in the Making
The Making of a Man
A Touch of Christmas

Richard Exley's books are available
from your local bookstore or from:

Honor Books • P. O. Box 55388 • Tulsa, OK 74155

To contact the author, write:
Richard Exley
P. O. Box 54744
Tulsa, Oklahoma 74155

Please include your prayer requests when you write.